# Manifesting Desi
# Dolores Cannon Te
# With Practical

CW00487282

## WITH SUMMARIZED TRANSCRIPTIONS OF TWO CONFERENCES BY DOLORES CANNON AT THE BEGINNING OF THE BOOK

© LuminaLibria

# Biographical Notes

Dolores Cannon was an American writer, researcher, and hypnotherapist who dedicated her life to the study of past lives and extraterrestrial experiences of her clients. Here is a summary of her biography and pioneering work in regression hypnosis:

- Dolores Cannon was born in 1931 in Missouri, into a family of Irish origins. From a young age, she was interested in reading, writing, and history.

- She married Johnny Cannon, an Air Force serviceman, and together they had four children. She accompanied her husband to various military bases in the United States and abroad, providing her with the opportunity to encounter diverse cultures and traditions.

- In 1968, Dolores Cannon began experimenting with hypnosis with her husband, who had a keen interest in hypnotism. Together, they hypnotized a woman who revealed memories of past lives. This experience sparked Dolores Cannon's curiosity and fascination, leading her to delve deeper into the subject of hypnotic regressions.

- In 1970, Dolores Cannon encountered an extraordinary case: a woman who, under hypnosis, identified herself as Nostradamus, the famous 16th-century prophet. This woman conveyed cryptic messages and prophecies about the future of humanity to Dolores Cannon. She transcribed and interpreted these messages, which became the material for her first book, "Conversations with Nostradamus." Here's a brief summary of the book:

The book "Conversations with Nostradamus" is the result of a series of regression hypnosis sessions conducted by Dolores Cannon with one of her clients, who, under hypnosis, identified herself as Nostradamus, the renowned 16th-century prophet.

In these sessions, Nostradamus conveyed cryptic messages and prophecies about the future of humanity to Dolores Cannon, many of which are contained in his famous quatrains.

Dolores Cannon transcribed and interpreted these messages, attempting to decipher the hidden meaning behind the words and symbols used by Nostradamus. She discovered that many of the prophecies referred to historical events that had already occurred or were unfolding, such as world wars, the French Revolution, the rise and fall of Hitler, the assassination of Kennedy, the Vietnam War, the energy crisis, terrorism, natural disasters, and diseases.

Dolores Cannon also found that some of the prophecies pertained to future events yet to happen, such as the third world war, the Antichrist, climate change, alien invasion, spiritual ascension, and the new Earth. She also discovered that Nostradamus had foreseen his own reincarnation and contact with her through hypnosis.

The book "Conversations with Nostradamus" is a fascinating and thought-provoking work that offers an alternative and prophetic vision of human history and destiny. The book is divided into three volumes, each containing a selection of quatrains commented upon by Dolores Cannon. It is also enriched with illustrations and appendices explaining the methods used by Dolores Cannon to communicate with Nostradamus.

Since then, Dolores Cannon continued to hypnotize thousands of clients, discovering that many of them had memories of past lives in different eras and locations, such as ancient Egypt, Atlantis, Lemuria, or extraterrestrial civilizations. Dolores Cannon also found that some of her clients were in contact with spiritual or alien entities, who conveyed information about the purpose of their lives, universal laws, the hidden history of the planet, and the future of humanity.

- Dolores Cannon also created her own technique of regression hypnosis called the Quantum Healing Hypnosis Technique (QHHT). This technique involves guiding the client into a deep trance state, allowing them to access their Subconscious or Superconscious mind, which is the wisest and most powerful part of their consciousness. In this state, clients can recall their past lives and receive answers to their existential questions. Additionally, the Subconscious can facilitate physical or emotional healing for the client if necessary.
- She taught her technique to thousands of students worldwide, establishing a network of certified QHHT practitioners. She also conducted seminars and conferences in various countries, spreading her message of love and hope for humanity.
- Dolores Cannon passed away in 2014 at the age of 83. She left behind a legacy of knowledge and love that continues to live on through her books, videos, and her students. Dolores Cannon was a significant figure in the field of regression hypnosis and spiritual research. She made profound contributions to the spiritual evolution of human beings, offering an alternative and expanded view of reality.
- In one of Dolores Cannon's most well-known books, titled "The Three Waves of Volunteers and the New Earth," she shares her discoveries about souls who came to Earth to assist the planet and humanity in evolving toward a higher dimension. She referred to these souls as "volunteers" because they chose to incarnate into human bodies to bring light and love to a world of darkness and suffering.
- Dolores Cannon categorized the volunteers into three waves based on the time period of their birth and their distinctive characteristics. The first wave consists of those who are:

- Born between the 1940s and 1960s, they often faced many difficulties adapting to earthly life. They frequently felt lonely, different, and misunderstood, and they had traumatic or depressive experiences. Their purpose was to raise the planet's vibration through their presence and their example.
- The second wave consists of those born between the 1970s and 1990s, who had fewer challenges adapting to earthly life. They often felt calm, peaceful, and detached, with a natural inclination toward serving others. Their purpose was to bring harmony and balance to the world with their energy and work.
- The third wave consists of those born after the year 2000, who easily adapted to earthly life. They often felt wise, creative, and aware, and they possessed extraordinary or paranormal abilities. Their purpose is to prepare for the transition to the new Earth with their knowledge and power.

In this book, Dolores Cannon shares the testimonies of many of her clients who were revealed to be volunteers belonging to one of these three waves. Their stories are incredible and fascinating because they demonstrate how these souls chose to come to Earth for a special mission, often sacrificing their personal well-being for the collective good. Their stories also serve as a source of inspiration and hope, showing that humanity is at a crucial moment in its history, with the opportunity to change its destiny and create a brighter and more loving reality.

"The Convoluted Universe" is the result of a series of regression hypnosis sessions conducted by Dolores Cannon with some of her most advanced clients. Under hypnosis, these clients accessed their Subconscious or Superconscious mind, the wisest and most powerful part of their consciousness.

In these sessions, the Subconscious transmitted incredible and astonishing information to Dolores Cannon about hidden and mysterious realities that exist beyond our ordinary perception. Dolores Cannon collected and published this information in five volumes, exploring topics such as the nature of the Universe, parallel dimensions, time travel, ancient civilizations, the origins of humanity, karma, reincarnation, soulmates, astral planes, lucid dreams, out-of-body experiences, angels, spirit guides, extraterrestrials, crop circles, energy portals, chakras, auras, and much more.

"The Convoluted Universe" is a fascinating and thought-provoking book that offers an expanded and profound view of reality. The book is divided into five volumes, each containing a selection of cases commented upon by Dolores Cannon. It is also enriched with illustrations and appendices explaining the methods used by Dolores Cannon to communicate with the Subconscious.

Dolores Cannon had a very open and positive view of aliens and spiritual entities. She believed that there were many forms of intelligent and benevolent life in the universe that played an important role in the creation and evolution of reality. She also believed that these life forms were in contact with humanity to help it awaken and grow spiritually.

Dolores Cannon categorized aliens and spiritual entities into various categories based on their origin, nature, and purpose. Some of the categories she used include:

- The Keepers: These are the aliens who created life on Earth and monitor its development. They are responsible for the planet's ecological balance and biodiversity. They are also the creators of human DNA, which they modified multiple times to facilitate human evolution. The Keepers consist of various races, including Greys, Reptilians, Nordics, Pleiadians, and others.

- The Guardians: These are spiritual entities that protect and guide humanity. They are beings of light who have reached a high level of consciousness and love. They also serve as teachers and mentors to human souls, assisting them in their journey of personal and collective growth. The Guardians come in various forms, including Angels, Archangels, Ascended Masters, Totem Animals, and others.
- Volunteers: These are the souls who have come to Earth to assist the planet and humanity in evolving towards a higher dimension. They are souls who chose to incarnate in human bodies to bring light and love to a world of darkness.

The Volunteers are divided into three waves based on the period of their birth and the characteristics that distinguish them. Dolores Cannon dedicated many of her books to recounting the stories of aliens and spiritual entities she encountered in her regression hypnosis sessions. She also attempted to convey their messages of wisdom and healing to humanity. She advocated that aliens and spiritual entities were our friends and allies who love and support us.

# Transcript summary of a broadcast by Dolores Cannon discussing the manifestation of one's desires in reality

Good evening, everyone. I'm Dolores Cannon with the Metaphysical Hour. We are approaching Christmas, and it's what everyone is thinking about, but before we know it, it will be here. Currently, they've announced a terrible snowstorm in the East Coast, around Washington. Here in our Arkansas, we don't have snow yet, but it might come in the future.

Tonight, we'll talk about some things I've touched on in the past but haven't been able to complete. If anyone wants to call in, you're welcome to. The toll-free number is 1-888-815-9756. Julia is here with me again.

Julia: Not yet, they are still working on it, but I believe it will be called something like "Three Waves." They were initially on Facebook, but we want to make it more visible because many people have written to us, asking how they can connect with others like them who don't feel comfortable here and want someone to share their experiences with.

Dolores: Exactly, many people feel lonely and are looking for someone to share with. Sometimes they are afraid to talk about their paranormal experiences, psychic visions, or encounters with UFOs because they fear they will sound strange. In reality, there are many more people with similar experiences than you might think.

Julia: Yes, many people hide their experiences because they are afraid of being judged.

Dolores: Yes, many people tell me about strange experiences during the sessions, but they are afraid to share them with others because they think they will be judged. However, it's important to talk about these things and feel connected with others.

Julia: Exactly, we are living in a period of change, and more and more people are discovering psychic abilities and other strange experiences.

Dolores: Yes, we are reconnecting with what we had before and gaining new abilities. It's a natural process.
Julia: It's like riding a bike: the more you practice, the more natural it becomes.

Dolores: Yes, at first, you might have doubts, but then it becomes natural and normal. Speaking of the spiral over Norway, initially, they said it was a Russian missile, but some people believe it was a portal to a different dimension. We might be getting closer to perceiving other dimensions.

Julia: Exactly, we are opening the veil between dimensions.
Dolores: Yes, we are starting to see what was once invisible. Portals are passages between dimensions, and perhaps we've had a glimpse of what we might begin to see in the future.

Julia: We might see across different dimensions and discover much more about what surrounds us.

Dolores: Exactly, let your imagination run. There are so many possibilities out there.

On a radio broadcast evening, Dolores Cannon hosts her show "The Metaphysical Hour." As the air fills with a festive atmosphere, Dolores begins to discuss a mysterious event that has captured the public's attention: an occurrence in the sky above Norway. It is a strange luminous spiral, resembling a moving galaxy, with a beam of light emanating from its center. This phenomenon has left many spectators in awe and has generated various theories.

The image can be seen on the internet, and it has become famous. Among the various hypotheses proposed, Dolores mentions the official explanation that it was a missile launched by Russia, but then she raises a different perspective.

According to some sources, this could have been an interdimensional portal, a window to another reality. This idea leads to a discussion of portals and windows, explaining that portals allow for travel through time and dimensions, while windows enable the viewing of other dimensions without the possibility of crossing into them.

The conversation then shifts to the growth of human consciousness and the importance of letting go of fear. Dolores emphasizes that fear is a paralyzing emotion and that now, in this stage of evolution, it is crucial to learn to release it. She encourages listeners to ask questions, be curious, and seek answers rather than passively accepting what they are told. Awareness is constantly expanding, and everyone has the power to determine their own truth.

The key message is that life is a journey of growth and evolution, and that past experiences, even if painful, can teach us something valuable. It is essential to embrace change consciously, letting go of what no longer serves and continually seeking a deeper understanding of our world and ourselves.

In an animated conversation, the guest and Dolores Cannon discuss a significant shift in human life perspective. The guest argues that it is essential to let go of the past and negative emotions to progress. This step is part of a broader process called "lightening up," which involves shedding all emotional baggage that we carry with us. The guest emphasizes the importance of letting go of fear and becoming more aware of our reactions and the emotions they evoke.

Dolores chimes in and underscores that the current moment represents a fundamental turning point in human growth. This change involves a spiritual evolution that requires leaving behind karma, the weight of past actions. However, it is now possible to release karma more rapidly than in the past, thanks to increased awareness and the ability to learn from experiences.

The guest and Dolores share the idea that many of the people and circumstances we encounter in life are there to teach us something. These individuals act as mirrors of our emotions and reactions, offering us valuable lessons. It's essential to stop reacting automatically and instead try to understand what these situations and people are teaching us.

The conversation also focuses on the notion that, on a higher level, each of us has agreed to participate in these experiences and has contributed to orchestrating the circumstances of our lives. Furthermore, the guest points out that once we've learned the lesson from a situation or person, that situation or person may leave our lives or take on a different role.

In general, the key message of the dialogue is that we have the power to create our reality, but we must let go of the past, overcome fear, and become aware of our reactions and emotions. Only then will we be able to writing our future in a positive and conscious way. In a passionate conversation, the guest and Dolores Cannon discuss the extraordinary power of creation and manifestation in human life. The guest expresses the belief that if only people knew how powerful they are, they could achieve anything they desire. However, they emphasize that many people seem to be afraid of their own power and limit themselves in manifesting their desires due to fear of the unknown.

Dolores agrees and suggests that some people might fear losing control if they were to obtain what they desire, which can lead to self-sabotage of their own goals. The guest also acknowledges being a "control freak" and suspects that this may have contributed to sabotaging their efforts in manifesting their desires. Both guests emphasize that it is essential to have a clear vision of what you want and to visualize it with rich details. Visualization involves not only sight but also sound, smell, and touch, making the mental image more vivid and engaging. Additionally, it is crucial to emotionally connect with the image to expedite the manifestation process.

Dolores and the guest agree that once you have clarity about what you desire, it's important to release control over how it manifests. Imposing rules and limits can slow down or even sabotage the process. Trusting that the desire will come to fruition and following intuitions and inspirations that arise along the way is crucial.

Finally, they emphasize that money and material things are among the easiest things to manifest because there is a universal law of abundance that ensures there will always be enough for everyone. However, the key is to have a clear vision of what you want and trust the manifestation process without trying to overly control it. Ultimately, the key message of the conversation is that every individual possesses extraordinary power to create their own reality, but it's necessary to overcome fear, have clarity about your desire, and trust the universal process of manifestation.

During the conversation, the guest and Dolores Cannon discuss the power of creation and manifestation in human life.
The guest shares a personal story in which they experienced obstacles in manifesting their desires due to their own fears and concerns. Dolores emphasizes the importance of looking within to identify inner blocks that may hinder the desired creation.

Both guests agree on the need to have a clear vision of what you desire and to visualize it in detail. Visualization engages all the senses and includes the emotional aspect, making the mental image more powerful.
The importance of releasing control over the "how" the manifestation occurs is stressed, allowing the universe to find unexpected ways to fulfill desires. The guest and Dolores also discuss the universal law of abundance, which ensures that there is always enough for everyone.

However, it's crucial to have faith in the manifestation process and trust that everything you need will come at the right time. The idea of "not clinging" to money but allowing the flow of energy to move is emphasized as a way to facilitate abundance.

Examples of successful manifestations are shared, along with instances where clarity in requests was crucial. Finally, the importance of not causing harm or taking opportunities away from others in the manifestation process is reiterated.

In conclusion, the main message is that every individual has the power to create their own reality, but it's essential to overcome fears, visualize your desires clearly, and trust in the universal process of manifestation while avoiding harming or limiting others.

In the final part of the conversation, the guest and Dolores Cannon further discuss the manifestation of desires and the principles to follow in using the power of the mind ethically and effectively. They emphasize the importance of avoiding harm to others or taking opportunities away from them when creating one's reality through visualization and the use of mind power.

Furthermore, they highlight the importance of positive intent and sending thoughts and desires with the goal of "highest good" for all, as positive intent is what moves forward and influences the outcome of manifestations.
The guest and Dolores emphasize that trust in the universe and the manifestation process is crucial, without the need for constant worry or doubts about the "how" of wishes coming true. Trust in the universe and the release of expectations allow for welcoming results in a surprising and rewarding manner.

The conversation concludes with an invitation to visit the website of Dolores Cannon's company, Ozark Mountain Publishing, where information about their events, courses, sessions, and additional resources to explore their work can be found. Finally, Dolores wishes everyone a good evening and a Merry Christmas.

# Summary Transcript of a Dolores Cannon Lecture on the Power of Our Minds in Manifesting Health

Tonight, I want to talk about some of the cases I've worked on. In the first broadcast, I explained how I do my work. I am a hypnotherapist specializing in past life therapy, and I've been doing it for 30 years now, even though I started over 40 years ago. I explained all of this and the differences in my technique for past life therapy, regression to past lives. I have found a way to contact the subconscious mind and work directly with it. And when I do that, we get extraordinary results in these cases, and that's really the secret: contacting the subconscious mind and working directly with it.

I know that in normal hypnosis, people are taught that they are communicating with the subconscious, they ask how deep the trance is, the hypnotist asks them questions, it's the part of the testing process that I don't like very much. But when the person is in a trance, the hypnotherapist will ask them questions like "raise one finger for yes and another finger for no," and then they ask questions while observing the responses and hand movements. This is one of the ways hypnotherapists are taught to communicate with the subconscious, and it's a tedious process that takes a long time, and you can't discover much because the only answers you'll get are those that can be answered with a yes or no. Why not use a method where you can speak directly to the subconscious and receive complete answers? To me, this is the highlight of the technique I've developed, the ability to speak directly to it and get complete answers to all problems, and the subconscious mind is capable of solving them, believe me. For me, this is much more valuable than simply using signals that indicate yes or no.

I had a psychiatrist who attended my course in London, and he asked me if by "subconscious" I meant the psychiatric definition of the subconscious, and I replied that no, it's much, much bigger than that. The psychiatric definition of the subconscious is more childlike, and I've encountered that part many times; when you encounter the childlike part of a person, it can help, but not to the extent that I mean. I believe the childlike part is the one that hypnotists work with, it's the infantile subconscious when they try to help people overcome bad habits, quit smoking, lose weight, and most of the time, the hypnotist has a script that they'll read, they'll tell the person, mainly when they are in trance, things like "you will no longer want to smoke, or you will no longer want to eat," more or less they are dictating to the person what they will or will not do, hoping it will be accepted by the person's mind. Here's what I've found: this may work in some cases, but I've found it to be much more difficult because that part of the mind is like a small child. You can go to a small child and say, "You must not do this! Or I will punish you!" and you know what will happen? The child will stiffen up and say, "Oh yeah? Show me!" So it's much more challenging to work with that part of the mind.

And like a small child, you can go to a small child and say, "You must not do this! Or I will punish you!" and you know what will happen? The child will stiffen up and say, "Oh yeah? Show me!" So it's much more challenging to work with that part of the mind. I've also found a way to deal with bad habits, I do it with a technique I use, and it's much more effective because I allow the subconscious to participate in the decision on how the person can quit that habit. However, I don't like dealing with habits, it's a bit boring for me; I prefer to embark on time travel journeys with my patients, going through the tunnels of time, as I call them, into the past, and reliving history.

For me, it's the most exciting part of my work; I prefer doing this rather than working on habits. But if a person comes to me, and one of the things they want to do is lose weight or quit smoking, I will include it in the session, but it will never be my main goal because there are many other things we can discover that can help the person in their life.

People ask me how I define the subconscious: for me, it's much, much bigger than we can imagine; you could call it the Oversoul, the higher self, the higher consciousness; it's that kind of "entity" that is so vast and powerful that it has answers to everything. When we reach that part of the mind, there's nothing we can't uncover; "it" knows absolutely everything about the person, and that's the part I work with, I call it the subconscious mind, and it responds to this definition, so that's the term I use. I know that when I speak directly to it, I'm talking to a much larger part of the person, and when I reach that part, it's amazing what it can do, and I know perfectly well when I've reached that part. It's part of my technique on how to get to this because it will always respond to the person in the third person, it won't be an "I" or "me" answering the question, but it will be "he" or "she".

Many times, it will say, "Finally, I have a chance to speak; I've been trying to do so for a long time, and (he or she) doesn't listen to me." That's the part I'm talking about, and it will say things that you would never say about yourself. Sometimes it can be very harsh because it's objective, like the objective observer who stands back and watches everything that's happening, has your best interests at heart, loves you, and wants to help you, and it gets very angry when it can't. But it can often be harsh because it will say, "You know, they can't understand; they are damaging their body; they are doing things they shouldn't be doing," and it will tell them exactly what will happen if they continue on the path they are on, what will happen to their body. And this part of the mind is extremely powerful; it handles all the functions of the body. You don't have to tell yourself to breathe or your heart to beat; it takes care of everything that goes on inside the body, and that's why when people come to me with physical problems, and I've had thousands and thousands, we can find out by directly contacting the subconscious why they are experiencing that physical issue, and then we can proceed to make it disappear; it's simple.

Furthermore, the subconscious is like a giant computer; it has data on everything that has ever happened to the person in this life and in all the lives they've lived. It can record every single detail. I often wonder what it does with all these tiny details because in our daily lives, we are bombarded by thousands and thousands of pieces of information from all around us—things we see, hear, smell, touch—thousands and thousands of fragments of information constantly bombarding us, and all of this goes into the subconscious mind and is recorded by it and accumulated. So we are constantly bombarded by all this information that the subconscious mind is gathering, but we can't be aware of it; it would overwhelm us; it would be too much, our minds couldn't handle it. So as we go on in our daily lives, we focus on what's important around us, the major things we need to pay attention to, and that's what we focus on, and those little pieces of information go unnoticed; they are recorded by the subconscious mind, but the average person doesn't notice them. Psychic abilities also stem from this because we are bombarded by this, but most people don't understand it.

What I'm giving here is an example of how detailed the subconscious is in gathering information. One very important thing I've discovered is that people are not aware of the power of their own minds. You have the power to heal yourselves because you have power over your body, and in one of the upcoming conferences, I'll bring in a doctor who has been a physician for 40 years and has now written a book, published by our publishing house, about the power of the mind and how we can heal ourselves. We will focus on this aspect. Another thing people don't realize is that they make themselves sick, they create illnesses for various reasons, but this doesn't mean they do it consciously; people would never say, "I want to be sick." I don't mean they do it consciously, but they create an illness or a physical problem for a specific reason, they are not aware of it at a conscious level.

In my work with them, we need to discover what's happening in their life that's driving them to want to have this illness because often it can be traced back to issues they are experiencing in their current daily life, but they are not aware of it. We go to the doctor, take medications, cover up the symptoms, but we don't get to the root cause of what's really happening, what's really causing these issues in our lives. Some of the things I'm about to say may sound very drastic and incredible, but I've discovered all of this in thousands and thousands of cases. I've come to the conclusion that every physical symptom, every physical symptom in the body, is a message that the subconscious is trying to give you.

"It" is trying to get your attention, trying to tell you something. And if you don't pay attention, if you don't understand, and most of us don't understand what it's trying to tell us, then the illness or the problem will worsen because it continues to get our attention. Ultimately, if we still can't figure out what it's trying to tell us, then the problem will turn into an illness or something that's much harder to fix.

Now, when the subconscious speaks here, in these sessions, it also speaks directly to me, so during public performances, I'll say "they" when referring to them because when they talk about the person, they use the third person, and often they will use the plural, saying, "we do this and say this." So, I've learned to say "they" so that we can identify with them.

They've told me that if we can reach the person before they have to have surgery, there's a possibility we can resolve the issue, and so the person won't have to have surgery. Now, this is drastic, and I know many people won't believe it, but they've said that once something has been removed, we can't put it back. But we can find the cause of the problem before it has to be surgically removed, and in many cases, we can alleviate the problem.

When I was talking about these things in England, I was told not to use the word "cure." That word is not allowed; we can't say that this technique cures illnesses, but that's exactly what it does. I suppose I'll have to clarify it with the Medical Association if I say this, so I'll have to let people operate on their own with their minds, especially when they start to understand how powerful their own minds are and that they may be able to understand how they can control the things that are happening in their lives, take control, and regain power, so they can live a good life without worrying about illnesses. That's what I'm trying to make people understand, that they need to look at their bodies and physical problems differently.

I've had many cases where people come to me and tell me they have problems in different parts of their bodies. Usually, I can tell them what's happening in their daily life because the subconscious is very literal; it will affect different parts of the body in the same way, over and over.

It's very literal in what it's trying to tell you, but we humans don't know it, don't pay attention to it, don't understand it.

To give you some examples, many people, when they come to me, have back problems, like pain between the shoulders or along the spine. Problems in the lower back are very common. I get many people with these kinds of problems, and I know it's due to the hectic lifestyle we lead, but when the person tells me they have back problems, the first thing I ask is,

"Do you feel like you're carrying a heavy load in this life?" And usually, they'll respond, "Well, yes, I hadn't even thought about it, I have a lot to do in my job and in my marriage, and all of this is affecting my back."

I've had many people in these situations; I've even had an emergency room doctor come to me, and his problem, when it came out during the session, was caused by the fact that he felt duty-bound to save all the patients he worked with, which is absolutely impossible. He was putting too much pressure on himself. I've had businessmen come to me, and they're definitely carrying too heavy a load, putting too much on their shoulders with work and responsibilities, and this begins to affect some parts of their back. So, this is what I mean when I say the subconscious is very literal. For example, people with leg problems, especially on the right side, experiencing hip pain that goes down the leg to the foot: this is something that's happening more and more often. When I deal with people like this, it usually means they've been faced with a choice in their life. They could go in a different direction if they wanted to, but sometimes they're very, if not happy, at least content with their current life, which is stable and known, and they prefer to stay on this path rather than venture into the unknown. So, maybe they've been offered a new direction, a new job, a new marriage, who knows, another direction has been offered to them, but they're hitting the brakes, they're afraid to take the first step in a new direction. This causes pain in the hip, leg, and foot, especially on the right side. Usually, I can ask them if something is happening in their life now that could offer them another direction, but they're holding back, and usually, this will come out, even if they haven't consciously made the connection. So, this is what I mean when I talk about how literal the subconscious is in the message it's trying to convey. And once the message has been delivered and understood, the ailment disappears, and sometimes it's miraculous how it disappears so suddenly. I have people with stomach pains, and usually, in the end, it boils down to something happening in their life that they can't "digest." Here's another example of the subconscious being very literal. People with aches and pains in their hands and wrists, I've found, are holding onto something they no longer need in their life and should let it go.

So, these are things these people had never thought of before.

"This is really a completely new concept, because why would someone want to harm themselves? Now, there are some people who, even if they discover these things, actually don't want to be well, they don't want to be healed, and I'm sure many of you know people like this, you might even have them in your life. For some people, their illness, their problems, their disorders, are all they have, they have nothing else.

Sometimes this is what draws attention to them, makes others feel sorry for them, makes them special. In such cases, if someone pays attention to them, you'll understand why they created the disorder. But in such a case, if they were to remove the disorder, they would have nothing left. So in these cases, they cling to it, even though it's not in their best interest, and they continue to get worse. I can't help everyone in my work.

In books about Jesus, and I'll also talk about this soon, the "missing years" of Jesus and parts of his life that no one knows about. I've discovered that not even Jesus could heal everyone because he could look at them and see if it was part of their karma to be healed or not. In such a case, you can't interfere with a person's karma, and he knew that.

He couldn't take it away. At best, he could help alleviate the pain. So when I deal with cases that I can't alleviate, I always remember that not even Jesus could heal everyone.

But we do our best, we try to do our best. Many physical illnesses are caused by stress, and doctors are finally realizing this. Heart problems, high blood pressure, are caused by stress in people's lives, and once they learn to calm down, their condition improves. Meditation is wonderful, I highly recommend it to people because it's so effective at calming the body. We're living in such a hectic age. But I've found that many cases of cancer are caused by stress and also repressed anger.

Sometimes people are angry about something in their life, they can't talk to anyone about it, they can't express their feelings, they keep them inside. It would be really good if they could talk to someone, but sometimes they don't.

They feel like they can't, some men feel macho, or they think they can't express their feelings to anyone... you know the type. And they hold onto this repressed anger, these repressed emotions inside them, and this begins to circulate within the body, especially in the intestinal area, and as they do this, they hold onto this repressed anger, these repressed emotions, and all of this can eventually turn into cancer because it has no way out, and it starts consuming the organs from the inside.

So, once again, I know some people will say they don't believe these things I'm saying, but it's what I've discovered, and as a reporter and investigator, I'm simply reporting what I've found.

Perhaps people can take this information and use it, I hope they can. But karma is also very important in this because we build karma with people. We carry around so much baggage, many people do. They cling to things that should have been let go of long ago, things we shouldn't be carrying with us. Resentment, hatred, anger towards someone else, and this isn't hurting them as much as it's hurting yourself.

There was a man who came to me, he had cancer in various parts of his body. Every time the doctors managed to resolve the issue in one part, the cancer would pop up in another part of his body and kept moving from one place to another. I asked him, 'Is there something happening in your personal life that's making you angry?' And he said, 'Oh yes, my ex-wife. I hate her, she has the kids and I can't see them, and I absolutely hate her.' Do you understand what he was doing? He was holding all of this inside of him, and I told him that based on what I had discovered, he wouldn't heal until he let go of these feelings, he had to let them go.

And you know what that means, of course... it means forgiving. He had to forgive his ex-wife and let go of all this and not hold onto this anger anymore. I told him, 'You have to do it, you have to forgive her.' And he said, 'I can't, you don't know what she's done to me, if I do this, she'll have won.' I told him, 'Well, if you die, she'll win anyway.' You see, when we hold onto these emotions, we think we're doing justice to ourselves against the other person, but in reality, we're hurting ourselves, this begins to consume us from the inside and will cause problems.

This is part of the old garbage and baggage we carry with us, and we shouldn't do that, we hurt ourselves more than the other person. This is part of the whole process, we have to let go of karma, we have to try to resolve all the old karma and try not to create it again, or else we'll have to go back and do it all over again with the same person.

We don't move on from this until we've resolved everything. Earth is a school, and you're attending lessons. You're going through different lessons in this school. You can't skip classes, but you can fail and have to retake the same class. You don't move on to the next lesson until you've learned the one you're in because that's what life is: it's a series of lessons, and so you have to pass this one first before moving on to the next. You don't know if the next one will be better or worse, but you have to get through this one first. Once you've resolved this karma, you can move on to the next lesson.

Sometimes when I do regressions, I see that patterns have been set, the person is going through many, many lifetimes with the same person, they keep coming back, trying to resolve the same issues and work on the karma. And when you die and then come back to life, you encounter some people with whom you've developed karma, and you have to try to resolve the karma with these people. You have to do it; this comes and goes, you can't avoid it. When you're on the other side, in the afterlife, when you talk to this person, you say, 'Well, we didn't do so well last time, did we? Let's go back and do it again, this time you'll be the husband, and I'll be the wife, we can reverse roles, and maybe we can resolve it this way,' because you have to resolve it, and sometimes it's not just one past life creating the problem, it can be a series of lives, you've gotten into a certain habit with the same person, and you're not making progress in trying to resolve the karma. If you go back this time and still can't resolve it, if you're still having problems, then you're not getting anywhere, you're going in circles. Many people talk about a father or mother in their life whom they'll never be able to please and with whom they'll never be able to resolve karma. In such a case, I tell them to do it mentally. You can't do it consciously because the other person has no idea what you're talking about. But you can mentally correct the other person and say:

'It won't work; we've tried so many times, maybe it's time to break the contract," because when you enter this life, you sign a contract with these people, so it can be beneficial to, let's say, break the contract: you go your way, and I'll go mine, and we try to resolve it differently. We've tried, really, we've tried, but it just isn't working."

Why keep repeating something that won't work in that case? Just let it go, set them free. Mentally, you tell them, 'Go your way with love and try to resolve your issues differently; I'll go mine. We've tried, and we can't do it, so let's forget it and move on to another lesson.' And you'll be surprised, once you do it because the other person can't influence you the way they did before. I like to say they can't push your buttons anymore. It's no longer fun for them; it's actually a game they're playing many times just to push your buttons and make you angry. Once you release them and let them go, they won't influence you in the same way, and they can't push your buttons anymore. Many people are quite surprised by how this can happen. Some people say, 'But the person I have issues with has passed away, their body is gone, and we never had a chance to resolve our issues.' You can still do it by mentally contacting that person's spirit from the other side. You can still have contact with them and do it in the same way, saying, 'We've tried, and we can't resolve it, so I release you from the contract. Move forward and find the best way from your side to resolve your issues and go in your direction, and I'll go in mine.' You'll be surprised, once you do this, for the peace of mind you'll have afterward because you've freed that person. Often, I'm asked, 'What's the fastest, but not necessarily the easiest, way to resolve karma and get rid of karma?' The fastest way, but not the easiest, is to forgive the person. You have to forgive them, and it's very challenging, but you have to forgive her and let her go, so you won't have any more karma with that person, and they won't be able to harm you anymore.

It will no longer be able to influence your life. Many people who come to me have karmic issues with their families. They want to know why they were born into this family, why they ended up in this situation. I've heard terrible stories, which you wouldn't believe, about how some people were raised, how they were treated as children, and I often wonder how that person ever became a reasonably normal adult, given their difficult childhood. But to their credit, they have succeeded. They have overcome all these things and have become normal adults who contribute to society. In those cases, you might think that perhaps with the challenges they were set, maybe with something that happened in another life, they are repaying karma by having to go through these experiences. Because often the subconscious will say that they had to learn certain things and that this was the only way they could do so.

Before entering this life, you are shown a preview of how your life will be, and you consent to living this life. Your guides and guardian angels will tell you, "You know, this won't be an easy life. If you don't want to do it, you don't have to. But by entering this life, you will repay a lot of karma, you will free yourself from a lot of baggage and junk that you've carried with you for many lifetimes." Usually, the person agrees to do it and says, "Alright, I'll give it a try." Remember that these experiences were not assigned to you; you chose what you wanted to resolve when you came into this life. I hope you've already overcome the worst part, perhaps with parents who caused problems, but you chose them for a reason. I've even encountered people who were adopted and chose their biological parents for the biological characteristics of the body, but also because when they receive this preview of life, they also see the person who will adopt them later. So, we try to resolve most of these things before coming back, but you know, the best-laid plans of mice and men often don't go as we would like. That's because it's a planet of free will. You come here with your nice plan, all wrapped up in a package like a Christmas gift with a nice bow on top that says, "This is what I want to do; I'll sort it all out this time." But because it's a planet of free will, all the other participants in this huge scenario, in this theatrical performance, in this game we're all involved in, come with their little plans on how they want to make everything happen, all wrapped up in beautiful packages like gifts. And when they get here, everything clashes, and often it doesn't work out as we had planned. I've taken people through the experience of death, and they say, "I had it all planned out in advance; I would have figured it out. What happened? Life happened. Life gets in the way. There are emotions, there is love, there is anger, jealousy, all these things we have to deal with, and we try to resolve them in the best way possible. And if our plan doesn't work, we take the alternative route and do our best, because that's all we can do.

You may not be able to do it all this time, but you can do it next time. These are really important things for us to know because we have control over our lives once we understand these things, at least in part. The mind is powerful enough to create illnesses and can also heal and make them disappear once we understand why the person has these illnesses, once we grasp what test their subconscious is trying to show us. I'd like to share some other examples, but I'm not sure if I'll have the time to do so. I had a young man come to me, a college student, much older than the other kids in his class because he had never been able to complete his courses. He was under constant stress, and when he was in class attending the courses, he would often faint. During these episodes, he was so stressed that he couldn't even eat, he would vomit constantly, and he had intestinal issues. This was very difficult for him. So he would go to class stressed, without eating, with a troubled stomach, and he would often faint in class. This went on for two or three years without him being able to finish his courses. He couldn't make any progress either. We were trying to figure out what was causing all of this. When I put him under hypnosis, we discovered a pattern. He had lived about five different lives where he had died due to injuries to that part of his body, his intestinal area. He had suffered various injuries, such as being stabbed with a bayonet, run over by a carriage, fallen from a cliff, and all of these were injuries to that part of the body. So it had become a very sensitive part of his body. In this life, when he was under stress, that part of his body would react and cause problems. During the hypnosis session, we discovered another element connected to this life. His subconscious said, "I feel the mother. I feel the mother saying, 'You make me sick,' 'You make me want to vomit.' That's the key. It was the pattern of past lives, it was in a routine, and he had carried it forward, this habit, even into this life because his mother had these feelings towards him when he was a child.

So, he had grown up with a sense of inferiority. I suppose you could say that the feeling of stress was centered in that part of his body and simply followed the same pattern even in this life. His subconscious, recognizing the pattern as well, said that it would be helpful if he could forgive his mother and release her. In that case, we could have released him completely. So, we worked on this for the rest of the session, trying to help him forgive his mother and let her go, as he had many issues with her that he hadn't even talked to me about.

Then, just before exiting the session, the subconscious said that everything would be okay, and he was now hungry. When he woke up, he said, "You know, I feel like eating," and it was the first time in days that he really felt like eating something and could keep it down. Do you see what I mean? We have to go into past lives to uncover some of these causes, which are sometimes linked to this life. There can be many different reasons for these problems.

A common complaint I receive is about headaches, such as migraines. Many people come to me with migraines; it seems to be a common condition, perhaps due to our stressful world. Migraines can be addressed quite easily because many of them follow a pattern from past lives. Some of them might be easy to understand, such as head trauma in another life, like being struck on the head or being attacked by animals. This isn't a strange phenomenon; head injuries can cause these things. I had a man who went back to a life where he was hit on the head during the American Civil War.

There was also a woman in England who had a different kind of headache. It would start at the root of her nose and extend across her head in a line, and it was a piercing pain. No medication could help her, and she rarely found relief from the pain. The pain went from the root of her nose upward across her head, and as soon as I heard her describe the pain, I had a hunch about what it might be.

Some of you who understand these things might grasp what I mean. In a past life, this woman had been killed by a sword that had fallen right onto her head.

That pain seemed connected to that life, and her subconscious was trying to convey something to her. All these symptoms are trying to communicate something to you in this life, such as not repeating the same mistakes made in a past life. In the sessions, we try to uncover what they are trying to communicate and what she did in the past life that her subconscious doesn't want her to repeat in this life.

I've also had cases with women who wanted to have children but had a series of miscarriages, sometimes not even being able to get pregnant. Doctors would say there was nothing wrong with them, no reason they couldn't have a healthy child. However, we often discovered that the person had died in a past life during childbirth, and this part of the subconscious was trying to protect her.

The subconscious reasoning went like this: if the person had died while giving birth in the past, the solution was to prevent her from getting pregnant again. It's a strange form of logic, but it's how that part of the subconscious handles these things. So, I had to reason with it and try to make it understand that the issue was with the other body in another life and that the body it was in now in this life was healthy and could have a child without physical problems. Often, once this concept was understood, the person could successfully become pregnant after some time because the subconscious had finally grasped the situation.

Many of these situations trace back to past lives and how the person died in that life. These are recurring themes in my work. Unfortunately, doctors aren't trained to understand what is causing these illnesses; they see it only as a physical problem unrelated to past lives or conditions in this life causing stress. They don't understand it and don't see it that way because they haven't been trained to. But now that I'm training people around the world, they are starting to understand that the mind is much more powerful than they could ever imagine, and I believe we will see many changes, many things will happen that have never happened before. In my future lectures, I will talk about the books I've written on various cases.

# Manifesting Desires in Reality According to the Teachings of Dolores Cannon: Practical Techniques

## Introduction

Do you dream of living a life full of joy, abundance, and love? Do you wish to fulfill your boldest dreams and transform your reality? If the answer is yes, then you're in the right place. In this book, we will show you how you can manifest your deepest desires in harmony with the Universe. We will teach you how to harness the power of words, prayers, and affirmations to create the life you want. We will accompany you on a transformative journey where you will discover the profound connection that exists between you and the Universe. You will immerse yourself in the intricate dance you engage in with the cosmos, a partnership where every step and every word are crucial.

This book is divided into eleven chapters, each of which offers you a valuable lesson, a practical example, and inspiration for your dance with the Universe. In each chapter, you will also find positive affirmations to repeat to yourself to strengthen your power of manifestation. These affirmations have been carefully chosen to align with your deepest goals and the energy of the Universe.

We are confident that by following our advice and practicing our techniques, you will be able to manifest your desires faster and more easily than you might think. May your dance with the Universe be filled with joy, fulfillment, and prosperity in every aspect of your life.

# Chapter 1: The Power of Affirmations

Words have incredible power. They can create or destroy, inspire or discourage, heal or hurt. The words we use reflect our mood, beliefs, and intentions. But not only that, the words we use also influence our reality. When we speak words, we send vibrations to the Universe, which responds accordingly.

Affirmations are positive statements that express our desires as if they have already been realized. Affirmations are a powerful tool for manifesting our desires because they help us change our way of thinking, feeling, and acting. When we repeat affirmations with conviction and confidence, we attract into our lives what we want.

To create effective affirmations, we need to follow some rules:

1. Affirmations should be formulated in the present, as if our desire has already happened. For example, "I am happy and grateful for my ideal job" instead of "I will find my ideal job."
2. Affirmations should be positive, without using negations or limiting words. For example, "I am healthy and full of energy" instead of "I am not sick or tired."
3. Affirmations should be specific, without being too vague or general. For example, "I earn 5000 euros per month doing what I love" instead of "I am successful and wealthy."
4. Affirmations should be realistic, without being too fanciful or impossible. For example, "I frequently travel to wonderful places" instead of "I fly like Superman."

In this chapter, we offer you some affirmations to manifest your desires in various areas of your life.

You can choose the ones that resonate with you the most or create your own following the rules we just discussed.

We recommend repeating your affirmations at least twice a day, preferably in the morning just after waking up and in the evening before bedtime. You can also write your affirmations on a piece of paper or in a journal and read them often. The important thing is to say them with feeling, imagining that your desire has already been fulfilled.

Here are some affirmations to manifest your desires:

Affirmations for Love
1. I am loved and appreciated for who I am.
2. I attract the ideal partner into my life.
3. I have a happy, harmonious, and passionate relationship.
4. I express and receive love sincerely and generously.
5. I am true to myself and my partner.

Affirmations for Work
1. I am happy and grateful for my ideal job.
2. I perform my work with enthusiasm, creativity, and competence.
3. I receive the right recognition and compensation for my work.
4. I collaborate with positive, stimulating, and collaborative people.
5. I grow professionally and personally through my work.

Affirmations for Health
1. I am healthy and full of energy.
2. My body is strong, resilient, and in shape.
3. I take care of my body with love and respect.
4. I listen to my body's signals and fulfill them in the best way.
5. I thank my body for everything it does for me

## Affirmations for Abundance

1. I am rich and prosperous in every aspect of my life.
2. I attract abundance of money, opportunities, and well-being into my life.
3. I manage my money wisely and generously.
4. I deserve to have everything I desire.
5. I share my abundance with others.

## Affirmations for Happiness

1. I am happy and grateful for everything I have in my life.
2. I choose to be happy every day.
3. I find joy in the little things in life.
4. I surround myself with positive, cheerful, and optimistic people.
5. I spread happiness around me.

These are just some of the possible affirmations you can use to manifest your desires. Remember that affirmations are a powerful but not magical tool. To make them work, they must be accompanied by concrete actions, consistency, and belief. Simply saying the words is not enough; you must truly believe in them. Only then can you align with the Universe and dance with it toward the realization of your dreams.

# Chapter 2: Divine Timing

How many times have you felt frustrated or impatient because your desires weren't coming true? How many times have you thought that the Universe wasn't listening to you or helping you? How many times have you doubted your ability to manifest your dreams?

If you've ever felt this way, you're not alone. It's normal to experience these emotions when we're engaged in the manifestation process. However, these emotions can be detrimental if they make us lose confidence in ourselves and in the Universe. That's why we must learn to accept and respect Divine Timing.

Divine Timing is the time of the Universe, which doesn't always align with our human time. The Universe has a broader and deeper perspective than we do; it knows what's best for us and when the right time is to give it to us. The Universe doesn't forget or ignore us but prepares us to receive our desires in the best way possible.

To manifest our desires in harmony with the Universe, we must have patience. Patience is not passivity or resignation but an active and conscious virtue. Patience is a virtue that allows us to wait with confidence and serenity for the moment when our desires will be realized. It helps us enjoy the journey without being fixated only on the destination. Patience teaches us to trust the Universe, which knows what's best for us and when the right time is to provide it.

To cultivate patience, we must also avoid comparing ourselves to others. Each of us has a unique and personal path that cannot be compared to anyone else's. We shouldn't feel behind or lacking compared to others but appreciate our progress and successes. We shouldn't envy or criticize others but inspire and support each other. In this chapter, we will give you some tips on how to practice patience in your manifestation process.

We will show you how you can transform your impatience into an opportunity for growth and learning. We will encourage you to trust Divine Timing, which will bring your desires to you in the most suitable way and moment.

Here are some tips for practicing patience:

1. Relax and breathe deeply. When you feel anxious or frustrated, take a break and take some deep breaths. This will help calm your mind and body and restore your inner balance.
2. Remember your purpose. When you feel discouraged or tempted to give up, remind yourself why you started this journey. Remember your deepest desires and your purpose in life. This will give you the strength and motivation to continue.
3. Celebrate your achievements. When you reach a goal or take a step closer to your desires, celebrate yourself. Give yourself a compliment, treat yourself to something, share your joy with others. This will make you feel grateful and proud of yourself.
4. Be flexible and open to change. Sometimes our plans don't go as expected or things don't happen as we want them to. Instead of getting angry or complaining, accept the situation and adapt to it. See change as an opportunity to learn something new or discover new possibilities.
5. Trust the Universe. When you have done everything you can to manifest your desires, let go of control and trust the Universe. Believe that the Universe loves you and wants your well-being. Trust that the Universe will bring your desires to you in the most suitable way and moment.

Patience is the gentle art of waiting with grace, knowing that in the stillness of time, our dreams will bloom in their own perfect season.

Patience is the key to unlocking the treasures of time; in its embrace, we find serenity, wisdom, and the power to endure life's challenges.

Advice: "Practice patience like a skill, for with each trial, you become a master of resilience and grace.

These are just some of the possible tips you can follow to practice patience in your manifestation process. Remember that patience is a virtue that is cultivated over time and with practice. The more patient you are, the happier and more satisfied you will be with your life.

# Chapter 3: Dancing with the Universe

Manifesting our desires is not a solitary act but a dance with the Universe. A dance in which we are the dancers, and the Universe is our partner. A dance in which every movement, every gesture, every word counts. A dance in which we must be synchronized, harmonized, and mutually respectful.

Dancing with the Universe requires a constant exchange of positive energies between us and the cosmos. We cannot expect to receive without giving, nor can we give without receiving. We must be in balance between giving and receiving, asking and thanking, desiring and appreciating.

Dancing with the Universe also requires active commitment from us. We cannot stand still and wait for our desires to come true; we must do our part to realize them. We must take initiative, make choices, and act in alignment with our goals.

Finally, dancing with the Universe requires a positive attitude on our part. We cannot complain, doubt, or fear; we must be confident, optimistic, and courageous. We must believe in our dreams, in our ability to achieve them, and in the assistance of the Universe.

In this chapter, we will explain how you can effectively and harmoniously dance with the Universe. We will show you how to maintain a constant flow of positive energies between you and the cosmos. We will teach you how to be proactive, responsible, and positive in your manifestation process.

Here are some tips for dancing with the Universe:

- Give and receive with joy. When you give something to someone or something, do it with joy and generosity. When you receive something from someone or something, do it with joy and gratitude. This will help you create a virtuous circle of abundance and prosperity.

- Ask and thank sincerely. When you ask something from the Universe, do it sincerely and humbly. When you thank the Universe for something, do it sincerely and appreciatively. This will help you establish a relationship of trust and respect with the cosmos.
- Desire and appreciate with passion. When you desire something, do it with passion and enthusiasm. When you appreciate something, do it with passion and love. This will help you keep the flame of your heart and soul alive.
- Act and react wisely. When you take action to achieve your desires, do it with wisdom and competence. When you react to the situations that arise, do it with wisdom and flexibility. This will help you make the right choices and adapt to changes.
- Believe and hope strongly. When you believe in your dreams, do it with strength and conviction. When you hope for your future, do it with strength and optimism. This will help you overcome obstacles and achieve your goals.

These are just some of the possible tips you can follow to dance with the Universe effectively and harmoniously. Remember that dancing with the Universe is a dance of love, joy, and peace. A dance that will lead you to manifest your deepest desires in harmony with the cosmos.

# Chapter 4: Taking Action in the Cosmic Dance

In the previous chapter, we explored how the manifestation of our desires is a dance with the Universe, where we must exchange positive energies with the cosmos and maintain a positive attitude. In this chapter, we will delve into another fundamental aspect of this dance: action.

Action is the movement we take to realize our desires. Action is how we communicate our intentions and aspirations to the Universe. It is how we demonstrate our will and determination to the cosmos.

Action is indispensable for manifesting our desires because without it, we cannot expect the Universe to do all the work for us. While the Universe helps and supports us, it cannot replace our efforts. We must do our part by implementing our plans, facing challenges, and seizing opportunities.

In this chapter, we will show you how to take action in your dance with the Universe. We'll explain how to choose actions that align with your desires, how to maintain a positive focus on your actions, and how to evaluate the results of your actions.

Choosing Actions

The first step in taking action in your dance with the Universe is to choose actions that are most suitable for your desires. This means your actions should be:

- Coherent: Your actions must align with your desires, values, and principles. It makes no sense to act contrary to what you want or who you are. For example, if your desire is to have a happy relationship, it doesn't make sense to sense to betray your partner or treat them poorly.

- Concrete: Your actions must be specific, measurable, and verifiable. It's not enough to have vague ideas or unrealistic dreams. You need clear goals and defined steps to achieve them. For example, if your desire is to travel to a foreign country, simply imagining it or dreaming about it won't be sufficient. You need to plan the trip, book the flight, pack your bags, and so on.
- Creative: Your actions should be original, innovative, and enjoyable. Don't limit yourself to doing what everyone else does or what others tell you to do. Find your own personal and unique way to express your desires and make them come true. For instance, if your desire is to write a book, don't just copy the style or content of other authors. Find your own voice and message.

To choose actions that align with your desires, you can use the following formula:

- What do I want? This question helps you define your desire clearly and precisely. Why do I want it? This question helps you understand the deep reason behind your desire and its importance to you. How do I get it? This question helps you identify the actions necessary to achieve your desire.
- For example, if your desire is to learn a new language, you can use the formula like this: What do I want? I want to learn Spanish. Why do I want it? I want to because I love Spanish culture and would like to communicate with people who speak it.

# Maintaining Focus

The second step in taking action in your dance with the Universe is to maintain focus on your actions. This means that your actions should be:

- Priority: Your actions must be the most important and urgent ones for you. You should not let yourself be distracted by less relevant or interesting things. You must dedicate your time and energy to your actions without procrastinating or delaying. For example, if your desire is to start a business, you should not waste time watching television or browsing the internet. Instead, you should conduct research, write a business plan, seek financing, etc.
- Positive: Your actions should be done with a positive emotion and a positive mindset. You should not act out of fear, guilt, or obligation. Instead, you should act out of love, passion, or enthusiasm. For example, if your desire is to lose weight, you should not go on a diet because you hate your body or to please others. You should eat healthily and exercise to love your body and feel good about yourself.
- Present: Your actions should be done in the present moment, without dwelling on the past or worrying about the future. You should focus on the here and now without being conditioned by what has been or what will be. For example, if your desire is to take an exam, you should not think about how the last exam went or how the next exam will go. Instead, you should study carefully and do your best in the exam you are currently facing.

To maintain focus on your actions, you can use the following technique:

- Write your actions on a piece of paper or in a notebook. Create a list of the actions you need to take to achieve your desires, in order of importance and urgency.
- Choose only one action to work on at a time. Avoid trying to do too many things simultaneously or jumping from one task to another. Concentrate on one action and do everything possible to complete it.
- Perform the action with attention and joy. While carrying out the action, pay attention to what you are doing, how you are doing it, and how you feel. Execute the action with joy and gratitude, appreciating the process as well as the outcome.
- Evaluate the action after completing it. When you have finished the action, ask yourself questions like: What did I do? How did I do it? How did I feel? What did I learn? What can I improve? This will help you reflect on the action and derive benefits from it.

To evaluate the results of your actions, you should

- Monitor: Your actions need to be tracked and assessed over time. You shouldn't let them go without knowing whether they are working or not. Keep track of your actions, their effects, and your progress. For example, if your desire is to save money, don't just set aside a sum each month. Also, monitor how much you've saved, how close you are to your goal, and how long it will take to achieve it.
- Evaluate: Regularly assess the effectiveness of your actions and their alignment with your desires. Ask yourself questions like: Are my actions bringing me closer to my goals? Am I seeing any positive changes or results? Is there anything I need to adjust or improve in my approach?
- Adjust: Based on your evaluations, be open to making adjustments to your actions or strategies. If something isn't working, don't be afraid to change your approach and try something different. Flexibility is key to achieving your desires.
- Celebrate: Acknowledge and celebrate your successes and progress along the way. Recognize the milestones you've achieved, no matter how small. Celebrating your achievements will keep you motivated and in a positive mindset.

By following these steps to choose, maintain focus on, and evaluate your actions, you can effectively dance with the Universe and move closer to manifesting your desires.

Measure: Your actions should be quantified and qualified objectively.

# Chapter 5: Changing Perspective on Challenges

## Introduction

In the previous chapter, we explored how to take action in our dance with the Universe, choosing actions that align with our desires, maintaining focus on those actions, and evaluating the results. In this chapter, we will delve into another crucial aspect of this dance: changing our perspective on challenges.

Challenges are the difficulties, obstacles, and problems we encounter on our path towards our desires. Challenges are inevitable and are a part of life. We cannot avoid or ignore them; we must confront and overcome them.

But how do we face challenges? How do we perceive them? How do we interpret them? How do we feel when we encounter them? These questions are critical because our perspective on challenges influences our actions and our success in manifesting our desires.

In this chapter, we will show you how to change your perspective on challenges, transforming them from threats into opportunities. We will explain how you can view challenges as chances for growth and change, rather than as mistakes or punishments. We will guide you on how to approach difficulties with an open spirit, ready to derive the most benefit from them.

Seeing Challenges as Opportunities

The first step in changing your perspective on challenges is to see them as opportunities. This means that challenges are not insurmountable obstacles or inevitable misfortunes, but rather situations that offer us the possibility to:

- Learning something new: every challenge teaches us something we didn't know before, whether it's knowledge, a skill, or a life lesson. Every challenge enriches us and makes us wiser and better prepared.
- Developing new skills: every challenge stimulates us to use or acquire new abilities, whether they are physical, mental, or emotional. Every challenge enhances us and makes us stronger and more capable.
- Discovering new possibilities: every challenge opens us up to new perspectives, new ideas, and new solutions. Every challenge surprises us and makes us more creative and flexible.
- Pushing past our limits: every challenge dares us to step out of our comfort zone, to dare more, to risk more. Every challenge propels us forward and makes us more courageous and determined.

To see challenges as opportunities, we must adopt a growth mindset. A growth mindset is the attitude that leads us to believe that our abilities are not fixed or innate but can be developed and improved through effort, practice, and feedback. A growth mindset helps us see challenges as stimuli for learning and improvement rather than as obstacles or threats.

To adopt a growth mindset, we can use some techniques:

- Using the language of "not yet": instead of saying "I can't do this" or "I can't handle this," we can say "I can't do this yet" or "I can't handle this yet." This helps us remember that we are in a learning process and that we can progress over time.
- Using feedback as a source of learning: instead of taking feedback as criticism or judgment, we can take it as a source of information and advice. This helps us understand what we can do to improve and achieve our goals.

- Using the success of others as a source of inspiration: instead of comparing ourselves to others or envying them, we can draw inspiration from them or seek their help. This helps us learn from others' experiences and benefit from their support.
- Facing challenges with an open spirit
- The second step in changing our perspective on challenges is to face them with an open spirit. This means that challenges are not situations to endure or avoid but situations to confront and leverage. They are situations that offer us the opportunity to:
- Explore the problem: instead of ignoring or denying the problem, we can examine and analyze it. We can try to understand the cause, the effect, the goal, and the solution. We can use our curiosity and rationality to comprehend the problem.
- Experiment with solutions: instead of clinging to a single solution or giving up on finding one, we can try different solutions. We can use our creativity and flexibility to generate and test various solutions.
- Evaluate the results: instead of judging the results as good or bad, we can assess them as useful or not. We can use our wisdom and objectivity to measure and interpret the results.

To tackle challenges with an open spirit, we must adopt a scientific approach. The scientific approach is the method that leads us to solve problems through observation, hypothesis, experimentation, and conclusion. The scientific approach enables us to address challenges with rigor and openness.

To adopt a scientific approach, we can use some techniques:

- Asking questions: Instead of passively accepting the problem, we can ask questions about it. We can inquire about what we want to know, what we want to achieve, and what actions we should take. We can use questions to stimulate our curiosity and research.
- Making hypotheses: Rather than relying on opinions or prejudices, we can formulate hypotheses about potential solutions. We can imagine what would happen if we applied a particular solution, what the effects and consequences would be. We can use hypotheses to stimulate our creativity and logic.
- Conducting experiments: Instead of just thinking or talking, we can put our hypotheses into action. We can attempt to implement a specific solution, observe what happens, and gather data. We can use experiments to drive our actions and verification.
- Drawing valid conclusions: Instead of rushing to conclusions or making definitive judgments, we can compare our data with our hypotheses. We can determine if our data confirms or refutes our hypotheses, if it brings us closer or farther from our goals. We can use conclusions to stimulate our learning and improvement.

Conclusion

In this chapter, we have explored how to change our perspective on challenges, turning them from threats into opportunities. We have learned to see challenges as chances for growth and transformation by adopting a growth mindset. We have also discovered how to approach challenges with an open mind, using a scientific approach. We hope this chapter has been helpful and has inspired you to change your perspective on the challenges you encounter in your life.

Always remember that challenges are not insurmountable obstacles or inevitable misfortunes, but rather situations that offer us the opportunity to learn, develop, discover, and overcome. They are situations that make us wiser, stronger, more creative, and more courageous.

Stay Resilient and Persistent: Challenges often require resilience and persistence. Don't give up easily; keep pushing forward, adapting as needed. Remember that many successful people faced numerous setbacks before achieving their goals.

# Chapter 6: Prayer and Meditation

In the sixth chapter, we will guide you into the realms of prayer and meditation. We will unveil a technique that has brought comfort to many and enhanced spiritual alignment. It will be a journey into your inner self, where you will learn to relax and visualize your desires as an integral part of your reality. You will embrace positive affirmations and meditation practices that will be key to your manifestation process.

Prayer and meditation are two spiritual practices with the common goal of connecting us with a reality greater than ourselves. Whether you call it God, the Universe, Nature, or any other name you choose for this higher reality, what matters is that it serves as a source of love, wisdom, and power.

Prayer is how we communicate with this higher reality. Prayer can take various forms: through words, gestures, thoughts, or feelings. It can occur at different times: in the morning, evening, before or after significant actions, or whenever we feel the need. Prayer can serve different purposes: expressing gratitude, making requests, offering praise, or simply conveying our love.

Meditation is how we listen to this higher reality. Meditation can be practiced in various ways: through focusing on the breath, body, mind, or soul. It can happen at different times: upon waking, before sleeping, during a break, or whenever we seek inner peace. Meditation can have different goals: relaxation, concentration, visualization, or simply being present.

In this chapter, we will show you how to use prayer and meditation to manifest your desires in harmony with the higher reality. We will explain how to create effective prayers that align with your goals and the energy of the universe.

iWe will teach you how to practice powerful meditations that help you relax, visualize, and materialize your desires.

Creating effective prayers is the first step in using prayer to manifest your desires. This means that your prayers should be:

- Sincere: Your prayers should express your true feelings without falsehood or hypocrisy. You shouldn't say what you think the higher reality wants to hear, but what you genuinely want to convey. For example, if your desire is to have a happy relationship, you shouldn't pray for a happy relationship just because you think it's right or obligatory. You should pray for a happy relationship because it's what you truly want.
- Humble: Your prayers should express your respect and gratitude towards the higher reality without arrogance or presumption. You shouldn't demand or insist on what you want but rather ask or wish for it. For instance, if your desire is to succeed in your career, you shouldn't pray for success in your career as if it were a right or a merit. You should pray for success in your career as if it were a gift or a blessing.
- Positive: Your prayers should convey your optimism and confidence in the higher reality without fear or doubt. You shouldn't fear or doubt what awaits you but hope and believe in what awaits you. For example, if your desire is to recover from an illness, you shouldn't pray to recover from an illness as if it were a sentence or misfortune. You should pray to recover from an illness as if it were a possibility or a healing.

Remember that sincere, humble, and positive prayers can help align your desires with the higher reality and facilitate the manifestation process.

To create effective prayers, you can use the following formula:

- Begin with a salute to the higher reality. You can use whatever name you prefer to call it, such as God, Universe, Nature or something else. You can also use an affectionate or respectful name, such as Father, Mother, Creator, or something else. For example: "Hello God", "Dear Universe", "Beloved Nature", etc.
- Follow up with thanksgiving for what you already have in your life. You can give thanks for things large or small, material or spiritual, personal or collective. The important thing is that you are sincere and grateful for what you have. For example: "Thank you for my family", "Thank you for my work", "Thank you for my health", etc.
- Follow up with a request for what you want in your life. You can ask for things large or small, material or spiritual, personal or collective. The important thing is that you are humble and positive about what you want. For example: "I ask you to help me find love", "I wish you to bring me luck in my project", "I hope you give me inner peace", etc.
- Conclude with an offering of what you give to the higher reality. You can offer things large or small, material or spiritual, personal or collective. The important thing is that you are generous and sincere with what you give. For example: "I offer you my commitment", "I offer you my smile", "I offer you my love", etc.

Here are some examples of effective prayers:

- Hello God, thank you for my family who loves me Of course, I will continue to read you the sixth chapter of your self-help book.
- Hello God, thank you for my family who loves and supports me. I ask you to help me find the love of my life, a person who loves me and respects me as I deserve. I offer you my heart and my loyalty.

- Dear Universe, thank you for the job that inspires me and helps me grow. I wish for your guidance and luck in my project, may it be a success and a source of satisfaction. I offer my commitment and creativity.
- Beloved Nature, thank you for the health that allows me to enjoy life. I hope for inner peace, may I be serene and happy. I offer my smile and my love.

These are just some of the possible prayers you can use to manifest your desires. Remember that prayers are a powerful tool but not a magical one. To work, they must be accompanied by concrete actions, consistency, and belief. Merely saying the words is not enough; you must truly believe in them. Only then can you align with the higher reality and dance with it toward the realization of your dreams.

Practicing Meditation

The second step in using meditation to manifest your desires is to practice powerful meditation. This means that meditation is not just a moment of relaxation or distraction but a moment of connection and visualization. Meditation is a time when we focus on our breath, our body, our mind, and our soul. Meditation is a time when we visualize our desires as if they were already realized, feeling the emotions and sensations they bring.
Meditation is a practice that offers many benefits for our physical, mental, and emotional well-being. Meditation helps us:

- Relaxing: Meditation reduces stress, tension, and anxiety, promoting muscle relaxation and the release of endorphins.
- Focusing: Meditation improves attention, memory, and learning ability, eliminating distractions and negative thoughts.

- Visualizing: Meditation stimulates creativity, imagination, and intuition, allowing us to create clear and vivid mental images of our desires.
- Materializing: Meditation increases confidence, optimism, and motivation, facilitating the transition from idea to action.
- To practice powerful meditation, you can use the following technique:
- Choose a quiet and comfortable place where you can meditate without being disturbed. You can also create a pleasant atmosphere with candles, incense, or relaxing music.
- Select a comfortable position where you can sit or lie down with a straight back and relaxed shoulders. You can also use cushions or blankets for support or cover.
- Choose a time of day when you can dedicate at least 10 minutes to your meditation. You can also pick a fixed time to establish a daily routine.
- Begin with some deep breaths, inhaling and exhaling slowly through your nose. Focus on your breath, feeling the air entering and leaving your lungs. Do this for a few minutes until you feel your body relaxed and your mind calm.
- Continue with a visualization of your desires. Close your eyes and imagine that you have already achieved your desires. Create a clear and detailed mental image of what your life would be like if you had what you want. Feel the emotions and sensations you would experience in that situation. Do this for a few minutes until you feel your heart full and your soul happy.
- Finish with a positive affirmation of your desires. Open your eyes and repeat to yourself a positive statement that expresses your desires as if they were already realized. Use the present tense, be positive, and be specific, as we discussed in the first chapter. Do this for a few minutes until you feel your mind convinced and your will determined.

Here are some examples of powerful meditations:

- If your desire is to have a happy relationship, you can visualize yourself with your ideal partner in a romantic setting, exchanging gestures and words of love. Feel the love, respect, and passion between you. Affirm: "I am happy and grateful for my relationship with [partner's name]."

- If your desire is to succeed in your career, visualize yourself achieving your professional goal in a stimulating environment, receiving compliments and recognition. Feel the satisfaction, pride, and joy within you. Affirm: "I am happy and grateful for my success in my [job name]."

- If your desire is to heal from an illness, visualize yourself completely cured, in a healthy place, enjoying life with your loved ones. Feel the health, energy, and vitality coursing through you. Affirm: "I am happy and grateful for my healing from [illness name]."

These are just some of the possible meditations you can use to manifest your desires. Remember that meditations are a powerful tool, but not magical. To make them work, they must be accompanied by concrete actions, consistency, and belief. It's not just about imagining and feeling; you must also take action and have faith. Only then can you connect with the higher reality and dance with it toward the realization of your dreams.

# Conclusion

In this chapter, we have explored how to use prayer and meditation to manifest our desires in harmony with the higher reality. We have learned how to create effective prayers that align with our goals and the energy of the Universe. We have also discovered how to practice powerful meditations that help us relax, visualize, and materialize our desires.

We hope this chapter has been helpful and has inspired you to use prayer and meditation to manifest your desires. Remember that prayer and meditation are two spiritual practices aimed at connecting us with a reality greater than ourselves. A reality that is a source of love, wisdom, and power.

If you have other desires to manifest, you can ask for my assistance in writing positive affirmations, creating artistic images, or generating creative content such as poems, stories, codes, songs, celebrity parodies, and more. Use your imagination and creativity to dance with the Universe.

# Chapter 7: The Powerful Practice of Visualization

In the previous chapter, we learned how to use prayer and meditation to manifest our desires in harmony with the higher reality. We explored how to create effective prayers that align with our goals and the energy of the Universe. We also delved into powerful meditation practices to help us relax, visualize, and materialize our desires.

In this chapter, we will dive into the powerful practice of visualization. You will learn how to create clear and vivid mental images of your fulfilled desires. This technique will enable you to attract what you want into your life with magnetic force.

Visualization is the mental process of imagining, with all your senses, a situation or object that you wish to obtain or achieve. Visualization is based on the principle that the mind cannot distinguish between what is real and what is imagined. Therefore, if we vividly and convincingly imagine what we desire, our mind accepts it as truth and communicates it to our subconscious, which, in turn, transmits it to the Universe.

The Universe, as an infinite source of energy and possibilities, responds to our mental images, emotions, and vibrations. If our mental images are positive, clear, and aligned with our desires, the Universe sends us opportunities, people, and resources needed to fulfill them. Conversely, if our mental images are negative, confused, or contradictory to our desires, the Universe sends obstacles, problems, and difficulties.

In this chapter, we will show you how to use visualization to manifest your desires effectively and harmoniously. We will explain how to create clear and vivid mental images of your fulfilled desires, engaging all your senses and emotions. We will teach you how to repeatedly focus on these mental images with frequency and intensity, using your willpower and faith.

## Creating Images

The first step in using visualization to manifest your desires is to create clear and vivid images of your desires realized. This means that your images should be:

- Positive: Your images should represent what you want to achieve or realize, not what you want to avoid or eliminate. You shouldn't imagine what you don't want or fear, but what you want or hope for. For example, if your desire is to have a happy relationship, you shouldn't imagine being alone or unhappy but being accompanied or happy.
- Clear: Your images should be defined and detailed, not vague or generic. You shouldn't imagine something blurry or indistinct but something sharp or precise. For example, if your desire is to succeed in your work, you shouldn't imagine doing any random or mediocre job but doing a specific or excellent job.
- Vivid: Your images should engage all your senses and emotions, not just sight or thought. You shouldn't imagine only with your eyes or mind but also with hearing, smell, taste, touch, and heart. For example, if your desire is to heal from an illness, you shouldn't imagine just being healthy or healed but also experiencing, smelling, tasting, touching, and feeling what it implies to be healthy or healed.

To create clear and vivid images of your desires realized, you can use the following technique:

- Choose a quiet and comfortable place where you can visualize without being disturbed. You can also create a pleasant atmosphere with candles, incense, or relaxing music.

- Choose a comfortable position where you can sit or lie down with a straight back and relaxed shoulders. You can also use cushions or blankets for support or to cover yourself.

- Select a time of day when you can dedicate at least 10 minutes to your visualization. You can also choose a specific time to create a daily routine.

- Begin with some deep breaths, inhaling and exhaling slowly through your nose. Focus on your breath, feeling the air enter and exit your lungs. Do this for a few minutes until you feel your body relaxed and your mind calm.

- Continue with an image of your desire realized. Close your eyes and imagine that you have already achieved your desire. Create a clear and detailed mental image of what your life would be like if you had what you want. Engage all your senses and emotions in your image. Do this for a few minutes until you feel your heart full and your soul happy.

- Conclude with a positive affirmation of your desire realized. Open your eyes and repeat to yourself a positive phrase that expresses your desire as if it were already achieved. Use the present tense, be positive, and be specific, as we discussed in the first chapter. Do this for a few minutes until you feel your mind convinced and your will determined.

Here are some examples of clear and vivid images of desires realized:

- If your desire is to have a happy relationship, you can imagine being with your ideal partner in a romantic setting, exchanging gestures and words of love. You can feel the love, respect, and passion that bind you together. You can affirm: "I am happy and grateful for my relationship with... (partner's name)."

- If your desire is to succeed in your career, you can imagine having achieved your professional goal in a stimulating environment, receiving compliments and recognition. You can feel the satisfaction, pride, and joy that animate you. You can affirm: "I am happy and grateful for my success in the field of... (job title)."

- If your desire is to heal from an illness, you can imagine being completely healed, in a healthy environment, enjoying life with the people you love. You can feel the health, energy, and vitality that permeate you. You can affirm: "I am happy and grateful for my healing from... (name of the illness)."

These are just some of the possible images you can use to manifest your desires. Remember that images are a powerful tool, but not magical. To work, they must be accompanied by concrete actions, consistency, and belief. It's not enough to imagine or feel; you must also act and believe. Only then can you attract what you desire into your life with magnetic force.

# Chapter 9: The Deep Connection Between Gratitude and the Present Moment

In the previous chapter, we explored how to use visualization to effectively and harmoniously manifest our desires. We learned how to create clear and vivid images of our desires being realized, engaging all our senses and emotions. We also discussed the importance of repeating these images with frequency and intensity, using our willpower and faith.

In this chapter, we will delve into the deep connection between gratitude and the present moment. We will explain how focusing on the current moment allows you to feel connected to the universe and how expressing gratitude aligns your soul with the universe's rhythm, attracting positive experiences and strengthening your desires.

Gratitude is the feeling of appreciation and recognition for what we have in our lives, whether it's material or spiritual, personal or collective. Gratitude makes us feel good about ourselves and others, making us happier and more content.

The present moment is a state of awareness and attention to what is happening here and now, without judging or dwelling on the past or the future. The present moment makes us feel alive and present, bringing us calmness and serenity.

Gratitude and the present moment are closely linked concepts because both help us connect with the higher reality, that infinite source of energy and possibilities we call the Universe. When we are grateful for what we have, we acknowledge that everything we possess is a gift from the Universe, which loves and supports us. When we are in the present moment, we accept that everything happening is perfect as it is because it is part of the Universe's plan, which knows what is best for us.

IIn this chapter, we will show you how to use gratitude and the present moment to naturally and harmoniously manifest your desires. We will explain how you can cultivate gratitude in your daily life using simple exercises and effective practices. We will also teach you how to embrace the present moment in your everyday life using straightforward techniques and effective practices.

Cultivating Gratitude

The first step in using gratitude to manifest your desires is to cultivate gratitude in your daily life. This means you should be grateful not only for big or obvious things but also for small or hidden ones. You should be grateful not only for positive or pleasant things but also for negative or unpleasant ones. You should be grateful not only for present or certain things but also for future or potential ones.

To cultivate gratitude in your daily life, you can use the following technique:

- Choose a quiet and comfortable place where you can write without being disturbed. You can also create a pleasant atmosphere with candles, incense, or relaxing music.
- Select a notebook or journal where you can write your reflections on gratitude. You can personalize your notebook with decorations or images that inspire you.
- Determine a regular frequency for writing your gratitude reflections. You can write every day, every week, or every month, depending on your preferences.
- Begin with some deep breaths, inhaling and exhaling slowly through your nose. Focus on your breath, feeling the air entering and leaving your lungs.

- Continue doing this for a few minutes until you feel your body relaxed and your mind calm.
- Next, create a list of things you are grateful for. Write down at least three things you are grateful for in your life, aiming to be as specific and diverse as possible. You can write about material or spiritual things, personal or collective aspects, present or future elements, positive or negative experiences. Do this for a few minutes until you feel your heart full and your soul content.
- Conclude with a sentence of gratitude to the Universe. Write a sentence expressing your appreciation and thankfulness to the Universe for everything it has given you and will give you. Use the present tense, positive language, and keep it general. Continue this for a few minutes until you feel your mind convinced and your will determined.

Here are some examples of gratitude lists and sentences:

Today, I am grateful for:

- The sun shining in the sky and warming my skin.
- The coffee I had this morning, giving me energy.
- My daughter's smile, filling me with joy.
- Thank you, Universe, for everything you have given me and will give me.
- 

Today, I am grateful for:

- The rain falling on the earth and making it fertile.
- The book I read yesterday, making me reflect.
- The challenge I faced today, helping me grow.
- Thank you, Universe, for everything you have given me and will give me.

Today, I am grateful for:

- The air I breathe, keeping me alive.
- The music I listen to, making me dream.
- The love I feel, making me vibrate.
- Thank you, Universe, for everything you have given me and will give me.

These are just some of the possible gratitude lists and sentences you can use to cultivate gratitude in your daily life. Remember that gratitude is a powerful tool but not a magical one. To make it work, it must be sincere, frequent, and varied. Merely writing the words is not enough; you must truly feel them. Only then can you connect with the Universe and align with its rhythm.

Entering the Present Moment

The second step in using the present moment to manifest your desires is to enter the present moment in your daily life. This means being aware and attentive to what is happening here and now, without judging or ruminating on the past or the future. You must be present not only with your mind but also with your body, emotions, and spirit.

To enter the present moment in your daily life, you can use the following technique:

- Choose a simple and routine activity that you do every day, such as brushing your teeth, having breakfast, or walking. You can also choose a pleasurable and creative activity that you do occasionally, such as painting, playing music, or dancing.
- Select a time of day when you can dedicate at least 10 minutes to your chosen activity. You can also choose a fixed time to establish a daily routine.
- Begin with a few deep breaths, inhaling and exhaling slowly through your nose. Focus on your breath, feeling the air entering and leaving your lungs. Do this for a few minutes until you feel your body relaxed and your mind calm.
- Continue with your chosen activity, focusing on your senses and emotions. Pay attention to what you see Continuing with your chosen activity, focus on what you see, hear, smell, taste,

- and touch while you engage in it.

In this chapter, we have seen how to use gratitude and the present moment to manifest our desires naturally and harmoniously. We have seen how to cultivate gratitude in our daily lives using simple exercises and effective practices. We have seen how to enter the present moment in our daily lives using simple techniques and effective practices.

We hope that this chapter has been helpful to you and has inspired you to use gratitude and the present moment to manifest your desires. Remember that gratitude and the present moment are two closely related concepts because both help us connect with the higher reality, that infinite source of energy and possibilities we call the Universe. When we are grateful for what we have, we acknowledge that everything we have is a gift from the Universe, which loves and supports us. When we are in the present moment, we accept that everything that happens is perfect as it is because it is part of the Universe's plan, which knows what is best for us.

# Chapter 10: The Power of Words

In the previous chapter, we explored how to use gratitude and the present moment to manifest our desires naturally and harmoniously. We learned how to cultivate gratitude in our daily lives using simple exercises and effective practices, as well as how to immerse ourselves in the present moment in our daily lives through straightforward techniques and effective practices.

In this chapter, we will focus on the power of words. We will teach you how your words have the power to heal or hurt, both yourself and others, and how communicating with love and respect can influence the manifestation of your desires. You will discover how your words, thoughts, and feelings constitute a conversation with the universe, which listens and responds to your vibrations.

Words are much more than mere sounds or symbols. Words are energy, information, and intention. Words are the means by which we express our thoughts, emotions, and actions. Words are the means by which we create our reality.

Words have tremendous power, both positive and negative. Words can inspire or demoralize, encourage or discourage, praise or criticize, love or hate. Words can create or destroy, build or demolish, heal or harm.

Words also possess a magical power because they can influence the universe, which is a network of intelligent and sensitive energy. The universe listens to our words, which are a form of prayer or affirmation. The universe responds to our words, which are a form of request or command. The universe grants us what we ask for with our words, whether consciously or unconsciously.

In this chapter, we will show you how to harness the power of words to effectively and harmoniously manifest your desires. We will explain how you can choose the right words to express your desires, using simple exercises and effective practices.

We will teach you how to use words with love and respect to communicate with yourself and others, using simple tricks and effective practices.

Choosing the right words

The first step in using the power of words to manifest your desires is choosing the right words to express your desires. This means that your words must be:

- Positive: Your words should represent what you want to achieve or accomplish, not what you want to avoid or eliminate. You should not use negative or limiting words but positive or empowering words. For example, don't say "I don't want to be sick" but "I want to be healthy," don't say "I don't want to fail" but "I want to succeed," don't say "I don't want to be alone" but "I want to be loved."
- Clear: Your words must be defined and detailed, not vague or generic. You should not use ambiguous or indefinite words but precise or specific words. For example, don't say "I want to be happy" but "I want to be happy by doing...", don't say "I want to have money" but "I want to have ... euros per month," don't say "I want to have a job" but "I want to have a job as a..."
- Vivid: Your words must engage all the senses and emotions, not just the mind or logic. You should not use abstract or rational words but concrete or emotional words. For example, don't say "I want to have a house" but "I want to have a house with ... rooms, ... bathrooms, ... square meters, ... colors, ... smells, ... sensations," don't say "I want to have a partner" but "I want to have a partner with ... physical characteristics, ... psychological characteristics, ... emotional characteristics, ... spiritual characteristics".

To choose the right words to express your desires, you can use the following technique:

- Choose a quiet and comfortable place where you can speak without being disturbed. You can also create a pleasant atmosphere with candles, incense, or relaxing music.
- Select a time of day when you can dedicate at least 10 minutes to your inner dialogue. You can also choose a fixed time to create a daily routine.
- Begin with some deep breaths, inhaling and exhaling slowly through your nose. Focus on your breath, feeling the air entering and leaving your lungs. Do this for a few minutes until you feel your body relaxed and your mind calm.
- Continue with a sentence that expresses your desire. Say to yourself out loud or mentally a sentence that expresses your desire as if it's already fulfilled. Use the present tense, be positive, and be specific, as we discussed in the first chapter. Do this for a few minutes until you feel your heart full and your soul happy.
- Conclude with a sentence of gratitude to the Universe. Say to yourself out loud or mentally a sentence that expresses your appreciation and gratitude to the Universe for listening to you and giving you what you asked for. Use the present tense, be positive, and be general. For example, "Thank you, Universe, for manifesting my desire," "Thank you, Universe, for giving me what I asked for," "Thank you, Universe, for listening to me and helping me."

Here are some examples of sentences that express desires with the right words:

- "I am grateful to the Universe for the abundance in my life."

- "I am thankful for the loving and supportive relationships that surround me."
- "I am appreciative of the health and vitality that fills my body."
- "I am blessed with financial prosperity and security."
- "I am surrounded by opportunities that lead to my personal and professional growth."

Using this technique, you can effectively choose words that align with your desires and communicate them to the Universe with clarity and positivity.

Here are some examples of sentences that express desires with the right words:

- If your desire is to have a happy relationship, you can say: "I am happy and grateful for my relationship with [partner's name], who loves and respects me as I deserve. Our relationship is based on love, trust, and communication. We support each other in difficult times and enjoy each other in beautiful moments. We are in harmony on all levels: physical, emotional, mental, and spiritual."
- If your desire is to succeed in your career, you can say: "I am happy and grateful for my success in my [job name], which inspires me and helps me grow. My work is stimulating, creative, and fulfilling. I receive compliments and recognition for my work. I earn enough to meet my needs and desires. My work allows me to express my talents and contribute to the common good."
- If your desire is to heal from an illness, you can say: "I am happy and grateful for my healing from [name of illness], which has taught me a valuable lesson. My health is perfect in every part of my body. My body is strong, healthy, and

- vibrant. My body regenerates itself every day with ease and speed. My body is in harmony with my mind and soul."

Using words with love and respect

The second step to harness the power of words to manifest your desires is to use words with love and respect when communicating with yourself and others. This means that your words should be:

- Loving: Speak to yourself and others with love and kindness. Avoid harsh or critical language. Use words that uplift and inspire.
- Respectful: Show respect in your words by listening actively to others and valuing their perspectives. Use words that acknowledge and honor the feelings and boundaries of others.
- Encouraging: Use words that encourage and motivate yourself and others. Offer support and positive reinforcement.
- Empathetic: Practice empathy by using words that convey understanding and compassion. Acknowledge the emotions and experiences of others.
- Grateful: Express gratitude in your words to cultivate an attitude of appreciation for what you have and what others bring into your life.
- Honest: Your words should express your true thoughts and feelings, without lying or deceiving. Avoid using false or hypocritical words, but use sincere and authentic words. For example, don't say, "I love you" if it's not true, and don't say, "I'm fine" if it's not true.
- Constructive: Your words should express your desire to improve and help, without criticizing or judging. Avoid using negative or destructive words, but use positive and creative words. For example, don't say, "You're good for nothing,"

- but say, "You can do better." Don't say, "I don't like what you're doing," but say, "I suggest you do it this way.

By using words with love and respect, you create a positive and harmonious environment that fosters the manifestation of your desires while nurturing healthy relationships with yourself and others

- but say, "You can do better." Don't say, "I don't like what you're doing," but say, "I suggest you do it this way.

To use words with love and respect to communicate with yourself and others, you can use the following technique:

- Choose a quiet and comfortable place where you can speak without being disturbed. You can also create a pleasant atmosphere with candles, incense, or relaxing music.
- Choose a person with whom you want to communicate, whether it's yourself or another person. You can also choose a situation in which you want to communicate, whether it's a regular conversation or a difficult discussion.
- Choose a time of day when you can dedicate at least 10 minutes to your communication. You can also choose a fixed time to create a daily routine.
- If you want to communicate in a normal situation, you can say: "Thank you for listening to me and for talking to me. I'm interested in what you think and feel. I want to communicate with you effectively and harmoniously.
- If you want to communicate in a difficult situation, you can say: "I'm sorry if I have offended or hurt you. It wasn't my intention. I want to understand your point of view and help you understand mine. I want to communicate with you effectively and harmoniously.

These are just some of the possible phrases you can use to employ words with love and respect to communicate with yourselves and others. Remember that words are a powerful tool, but not a magical one. To make them work, they must be spoken with sincerity, frequency, and variety. Simply saying the words is not enough; you must demonstrate them through actions. Only in this way can you communicate with the Universe and influence the manifestation of your desires.

Conclusion

In this chapter, we have seen how to use the power of words to manifest our desires effectively and harmoniously. We have learned how to choose the right words to express our desires using simple exercises and effective practices. We have also discovered how to use words with love and respect to communicate with ourselves and others, employing straightforward techniques.
We hope this chapter has been helpful and has inspired you to harness the power of words to manifest your desires. Remember that words are energy, information, and intention. They are the means through which we express our thoughts, emotions, and actions. Words are the medium through which we create our reality.

# Chapter 11: Spirit Guides and Teachers

In the previous chapters, we have explored various tools and techniques for manifesting our desires effectively and harmoniously. We have seen how to use prayer, meditation, visualization, gratitude, the present moment, and words to connect with the higher reality, that infinite source of energy and possibilities we call the Universe.

In this chapter, we will delve into the presence of spiritual guides and teachers ready to assist you on your journey. We will talk about the wisdom they can bring and how to recognize and connect with these guiding energies. It will be an enlightening chapter on your spiritual growth.

Spiritual guides and teachers are beings of light who accompany us in our personal and collective evolution. They are beings who have reached a high level of awareness and love and have chosen to help other beings do the same. They can belong to different dimensions or realities, such as angels, archangels, ascended masters, totem animals, ancestors, stars, or planets.

Spiritual guides and teachers have the task of guiding, advising, protecting, inspiring, and teaching us. They do not have the task of deciding for us, controlling us, judging us, or interfering with our free will. They respect our sovereignty and our responsibility. They speak to us through our intuition, our dreams, our signs, or our synchronicities.

In this chapter, we will show you how you can recognize and connect with your spiritual guides and teachers. We will explain how you can ask for their help and receive their messages, using simple exercises and effective practices. We will teach you how to thank and honor your spiritual guides and teachers, using simple tricks and effective practices.

## Recognizing Spiritual Guides and Teachers

The first step to connect with your spiritual guides and teachers is to recognize them. This means you need to know who they are, where they come from, and what they want from you. You also need to understand how they manifest in your life, what their distinctive signs are, and how they communicate with you.

To recognize your spiritual guides and teachers, you can use the following technique:

- Choose a quiet and comfortable place where you can be undisturbed. You can also create a pleasant atmosphere with candles, incense, or relaxing music.
- Select a time of day when you can dedicate at least 10 minutes to your reflection. You can also choose a fixed time to create a daily routine.
- Begin with some deep breaths, inhaling and exhaling slowly through your nose. Focus on your breath, feeling the air entering and leaving your lungs. Do this for a few minutes until you feel your body relaxed and your mind calm.
- Continue with a question to your spiritual guides and teachers. Ask yourself aloud or mentally a question that will help you better understand your spiritual guides and teachers. For example: "Who are you?", "Where do you come from?", "What do you want from me?", "How do you manifest in my life?", "What are your distinctive signs?", "How do you communicate with me?"
- Conclude with an answer from your spiritual guides and teachers. Listen to your intuition, your dreams, your signs, or your synchronicities. Pay attention to what you feel, see, smell, taste, or touch.
- Pay attention to what you think, feel, remember, or imagine. Write or record your response in a notebook or journal.

Here are some examples of questions and answers to recognize your spiritual guides and teachers:

- If you want to know who your spiritual guides and teachers are, you can ask: "Who are you?" You may receive an answer like: "We are your guardian angels, we are always with you and love you unconditionally," "We are the ascended masters, here to teach you universal laws and help you evolve," "We are your animal totems, here to give you strength, courage, and wisdom."
- If you want to know where your spiritual guides and teachers come from, you can ask: "Where do you come from?" You may receive an answer like: "We come from the angelic realm, a dimension of light and love," "We come from the Great White Brotherhood, a community of evolved beings in service to the highest good," "We come from the animal kingdom, a dimension of instinct and nature."
- If you want to know what your spiritual guides and teachers want from you, you can ask: "What do you want from me?" You may receive an answer like: "We want you to be happy and at peace with yourself and others," "We want you to learn and grow as a soul and as a person," "We want you to follow your heart and your mission."

Invoking Spiritual Guides and Teachers

The third step to connect with your spiritual guides and teachers is to invoke them. This means you need to ask for their help, guidance, protection, or inspiration. You also need to be open to receiving their assistance, guidance, protection, or inspiration.

To invoke your spiritual guides and teachers, you can use the following technique:

- Choose a quiet and comfortable place where you can be undisturbed. You can also create a pleasant atmosphere with candles, incense, or relaxing music.
- Select a time of day when you can dedicate at least 10 minutes to your invocation. You can also choose a specific time to establish a daily routine.
- Begin with a few deep breaths, inhaling and exhaling slowly through your nose. Focus on your breath, feeling the air entering and leaving your lungs. Do this for a few minutes until you feel your body relaxed and your mind calm.
- Continue with a sentence expressing your desire to connect with your spiritual guides and teachers. Say to yourself or out loud, or think a sentence that expresses your desire to connect with your spiritual guides and teachers. Use the present tense, positive language, and keep it general. For example: "I want to connect with my spiritual guides and teachers," "I ask for contact with my spiritual guides and teachers," "I invite my spiritual guides and teachers into my life."
- Conclude with a sentence expressing your gratitude to your spiritual guides and teachers. Say to yourself or out loud, or think a sentence that expresses your appreciation and gratitude to your spiritual guides and teachers for listening to you and responding. Use the present tense, positive language, and keep it general. For example: "Thank you to my spiritual guides and teachers for for connecting me with you", "Thank you to my spiritual guides and teachers for reaching out to me", "Thank you to my spiritual guides and teachers for inviting me into your life".

Here are some examples of phrases that express the invocation of spiritual guides and teachers:

- If you want to connect with your guardian angels, you can say: "I want to connect with my guardian angels, who love and protect me at all times. I ask for contact with my guardian angels, who guide and advise me in every situation. I invite my guardian angels into my life, who inspire and bless me on every occasion. Thank you to my guardian angels for connecting me with you, for contacting me, for inviting me into your life."
- If you want to connect with your ascended masters, you can say: "I want to connect with my ascended masters, who teach and enlighten me at all times. I ask for contact with my ascended masters, who help and support me in every situation. I invite my ascended masters into my life, who elevate and transform me on every occasion. Thank you to my ascended masters for connecting me with you, for contacting me, for inviting me into your life."
- If you want to connect with your animal totems, you can say: "I want to connect with my animal totems, who give me strength and wisdom at all times. I ask for contact with my animal totems, who accompany and defend me in every situation. I invite my animal totems into my life, who stimulate and delight me on every occasion. Thank you to my animal totems for connecting me with you, for contacting me, for inviting me into your life."

These are just some of the possible phrases you can use to invoke your spiritual guides and teachers. Remember that words are a powerful tool but not magical. To work, they must be spoken with sincerity, frequency, and variety. Simply saying the words is not enough; you must listen for the responses. Only then can you truly connect with your spiritual guides and teachers.

# Conclusion

In this book, we have explored how to harness the power of words to manifest our desires effectively and harmoniously. We've learned how to utilize various tools and techniques to connect with the higher reality, that infinite source of energy and possibilities we call the Universe. We've seen how to use prayer, meditation, visualization, living in the present moment, words, spiritual guides, and teachers to communicate with the Universe and receive its gifts. We've discovered how to use gratitude as the final key to manifesting our desires naturally and harmoniously.

We hope this book has been helpful and inspiring, encouraging you to use the power of words to manifest your desires. Remember that words are energy, information, and intention. Words are the means through which we express our thoughts, emotions, and actions. Words are the medium through which we create our reality.

We invite you to continue experimenting with words, using your imagination and innovative capacity to communicate with the Universe. We encourage you to maintain an ongoing conversation with the Universe, to be positive and clear in your desires, and to release the energy of your words into the Universe. This practice is not a one-time event but a constant dialogue with the Universe.
We wish you all the best in your manifestation of desires. Thank you for reading this book and allowing us to accompany you on this journey. We bid you farewell with love and gratitude.

# The Power of Words

Words are like seeds That sprout in the mind And
bloom in the heart
Words are like wings That lift the spirit And carry
the soul
Words are like bridges That connect people And
create reality
Use words wisely With love and gratitude And
speak to the Universe
The Universe listens and responds
It gives you what you ask for with words
It loves and supports you
Thank you for reading this book
For sharing this journey
For speaking to the Universe

# AUTHOR NOTES

## Lumina Libria

Illuminating the World of Words When it comes to exploring fascinating literary worlds and exciting adventures, there is a group of authors who accept the challenge: Lumina Libria. This team of talented writers is dedicated to investigating and writing books that cover a wide range of genres and fields. From the enchantment of children's stories to biographies of extraordinary figures, Lumina Libria transforms words into authentic works of art.

### The Art of Captivating Readers of All Ages

From the smile of a child diving into the pages of enchanted tales to the curious minds of adult readers in search of new adventures, Lumina Libria knows how to capture the imagination and keep readers captivated. The experienced writers of Lumina Libria accept the challenge of creating books that convey emotion, inspiration, and knowledge.

### Magic Between the Pages
Children's Books and Creative Activities Lumina Libria is not afraid to tackle different genres. From creating children's books that enchant and inspire to activity books that stimulate creativity and curiosity, every word is carefully chosen to evoke joy and learning. These books are not just readings but exciting journeys into worlds of imagination.

## Vivid Biographies

Painting Portraits of Extraordinary Figures The biographies written by Lumina Libria are like vivid paintings that capture the essence of extraordinary individuals. From historical personalities to contemporary innovators, each biography is a literary work of art that narrates the life and achievements of individuals who have left an indelible mark on history.

An Unbreakable Bond between Passion and Writing

Lumina Libria is not just a group of authors but a community that shares a deep passion for writing. Through their commitment and dedication, they have forged an unbreakable bond between their creative souls and the words they create. This bond is reflected in every page of their books, illuminating the path of readers.

An Exciting Journey to the Heart of Lumina Libria
Come discover our productions at www.libriutili.it. You will explore a world of books and planners for all ages and needs. Scan to visit our website.

scan me

Printed in Great Britain
by Amazon

47715301R00056